**4⏱minute**
BIBLE STUDIES

Living Victoriously in Difficult Times

Kay Arthur, Bob & Diane Vereen

PRECEPT MINISTRIES INTERNATIONAL

WATERBROOK
PRESS

LIVING VICTORIOUSLY IN DIFFICULT TIMES

All Scripture quotations, unless otherwise indicated, are taken from the New American Standard Bible® (NASB). © Copyright The Lockman Foundation 1960, 1962, 1963, 1968, 1971, 1972, 1973, 1975, 1977, 1995. Used by permission. (www.Lockman.org).

Italics in Scripture quotations reflect the author's added emphasis.

Trade Paperback ISBN 978-0-307-45767-7
eBook ISBN 978-0-307-55241-9

Published in the United States by WaterBrook, an imprint of the Crown Publishing Group, a division of Penguin Random House LLC, New York.

WATERBROOK® and its deer colophon are registered trademarks of Penguin Random House LLC.

Printed in the United States of America
2020

30 29 28 27 26 25 24 23 22 21 20 19 18 17 16

SPECIAL SALES
Most WaterBrook books are available at special quantity discounts when purchased in bulk by corporations, organizations, and special-interest groups. Custom imprinting or excerpting can also be done to fit special needs. For information, please e-mail specialmarketscms@penguinrandomhouse.com.

HOW TO USE THIS STUDY

This small-group study is for people who are interested in learning for themselves more about what the Bible says on various subjects, but who have only limited time to meet together. It's ideal, for example, for a lunch group at work, an early morning men's group, a young mother's group meeting in a home, a Sunday-school class, or even family devotions. (It's also ideal for small groups that typically have longer meeting times—such as evening groups or Saturday morning groups—but want to devote only a portion of their time together to actual study, while reserving the rest for prayer, fellowship, or other activities.)

This book is designed so that all the group's participants will complete each lesson's study activities *at the same time*. Discussing your insights drawn from what God says about the subject reveals exciting, life-impacting truths.

Although it's a group study, you'll need a facilitator to lead the study and keep the discussion moving. (This person's function is *not* that of a lecturer or teacher. However, when this book is used in a Sunday-school class or similar setting, the teacher should feel free to lead more directly and to bring in other insights in addition to those provided in each week's lesson.)

If *you* are your group's facilitator, the leader, here are some helpful points for making your job easier:

- Go through the lesson and mark the text before you lead the group. This will give you increased familiarity with the material and will enable you to facilitate the group with greater ease. It may be easier for you to lead the group through the instructions for marking if you, as a leader, choose a specific color for each symbol you mark.

- As you lead the group, start at the beginning of the text and simply read it aloud in the order it appears in the lesson, including the "insight boxes," which appear throughout. Work through the lesson together, observing and discussing what you learn. As you read the Scripture verses, have the group say aloud the word they are marking in the text.

- The discussion questions are there simply to help you cover the material. As the class moves into the discussion, many times you will find that they will cover the questions on their own. Remember, the discussion questions are there to guide the group through the topic, not to squelch discussion.

- Remember how important it is for people to verbalize their answers and discoveries. This greatly strengthens their personal understanding of each week's lesson. Try to ensure that everyone has plenty of opportunity to contribute to each week's discussions.

- Keep the discussion moving. This may mean spending more time on some parts of the study than on others. If necessary, you should feel free to spread out a lesson over more than one session. However, remember that you don't want to slow the pace too much. It's much better to leave everyone "wanting more" than to have people dropping out because of declining interest.

- If the validity or accuracy of some of the answers seems questionable, you can gently and cheerfully remind the group to stay focused on the truth of the Scriptures. Your object is to learn what the Bible says, not to engage in human philosophy. Simply stick with the Scriptures and give God the opportunity to speak. His Word *is* truth (John 17:17)!

LIVING VICTORIOUSLY IN DIFFICULT TIMES

Have you ever felt overwhelmed by your circumstances, believing no one else has ever suffered in the same way? Did it seem as if no one could possibly understand your pain?

Do you wonder why life so often seems unfair? Some people seem to get everything they want and never have any real problems, while others seem to struggle all of their lives, facing one challenge after another. Some seem to get away with inflicting pain on the innocent, without experiencing any punishment in return. Has God turned His back on His children who are suffering, or is there purpose in the pain? How can we face the injustices and suffering of this world while clinging to faith in an all-powerful God?

These questions and more will be addressed in our six-week inductive study, as we gain a biblical understanding of God's perspective of our struggles. You will discover how to respond when you find yourself in the midst of difficult challenges—and you'll find hope for enduring faithfully to the end.

Once we entrust our lives to God, are we exempt from the pain and difficulties of life? Does our relationship with Him provide protection against suffering? We will begin this week's study by looking at a group of people whose circumstances shed light on these questions.

OBSERVE

The passage we'll be reading was written by the apostle Paul to the church at Thessalonica.

Leader: Read aloud 2 Thessalonians 1:3-5.

- *Have the group circle each (you) and (your) that refers to the recipients of this letter.*

As you read the text, it's helpful to have the group say those key words aloud as they mark them. This way everyone will be sure to mark every occurrence of the word, including any synonymous words or phrases. Do this throughout the study.

DISCUSS

- What did you learn from marking references to the recipients of Paul's letter? How would you characterize their relationship with God? What was happening to them?

2 THESSALONIANS 1:3-5

3 We ought always to give thanks to God for (you) brethren, as is only fitting, because (your) faith is greatly enlarged, and the love of each one of (you) toward one another grows ever greater;

4 therefore, we ourselves speak proudly of (you) among the churches of God for your perseverance and faith in the midst of all your persecutions and afflictions which you endure.

5 This is a plain indication of God's righteous judgment so that you will be considered worthy of the kingdom of God, for which indeed you are suffering.

• How were they responding to their circumstances?

INSIGHT

The New Testament was originally written in the Greek language. The Greek word translated as *perseverance* in 2 Thessalonians 1:4 is *hupomone*, which means "patience or endurance in difficult circumstances." This word indicates the Thessalonians were not surrendering to their circumstances nor were they running away to get out of the situation.

The Greek word translated as *faith* in verse 4 means "to believe, to be fully persuaded." In this context it shows that their faith and trust was in God, who enabled them to accept their circumstances and cope with these trials.

Also in verse 4, the Greek word translated as *endure* is *anecho*, which means "to patiently wait." God gives the believer inner strength to enable him to be steadfast, to patiently wait in the midst of difficult circumstances.

• What additional insights did you gain from the definitions of these words regarding the response of the Thessalonians to their circumstances?

• According to these definitions, what enabled the Thessalonian believers to cope with their situation?

faith

• How does your standard response in difficult situations compare with that of the Thessalonians? If Paul were describing your faith, in what ways would his description differ from or be similar to this passage in 2 Thessalonians?

OBSERVE

Leader: *Read aloud 2 Thessalonians 1:4-8.*
  • *Have the group mark every reference to **persecutions, afflictions (afflict, afflicted),** and **suffering,** like this:*
  MMV

2 THESSALONIANS 1:4-8

4 therefore, we ourselves speak proudly of you among the churches of God for your perseverance and faith in the midst of all your persecutions and afflictions which you endure.

⁵ This is a plain indication of God's righteous judgment so that you will be considered worthy of the kingdom of God, for which indeed you are suffering.

⁶ For after all it is only just for God to repay with affliction those who afflict you,

⁷ and to give relief to you who are afflicted and to us as well when the Lord Jesus will be revealed from heaven with His mighty angels in flaming fire,

⁸ dealing out retribution to those who do not know God and to those who do not obey the gospel of our Lord Jesus.

INSIGHT

The Greek word for *persecutions* is *diogomos*, which means "hostile persecutions." It involves being pursued by enemies.

Afflictions is translated from the Greek word *thlipsis*, which means "to crush or to squeeze." It refers almost invariably to something that comes upon one from outward circumstances.

The Greek word translated here as *suffering* is *pascho*, which means "to be acted upon or to be affected by some outward circumstances."

Afflict and afflicted are translated from the Greek word *thilbo*, which means "to press or to be troubled." It indicates sufferings due to the pressure of circumstances or antagonism from others. To be afflicted is to be oppressed with evil.

DISCUSS

• Look back to where you marked each of the key words in the text and discuss what these definitions reveal about the pressures the Thessalonians were enduring.

• What truths did you learn from the circumstances and the example of the Thessalonians that you can apply to your life?

OBSERVE

Let's look at some other verses where Paul wrote about suffering in the life of a believer.

Leader: *Read aloud 1 Thessalonians 1:6-7; 2:1,2,14; and 3:4. Have the group do the following:*

• *Circle the pronouns **you** and **your,** which refer to believers in the Thessalonian church:* ⬭

• *Draw a box* ☐ *around the pronouns **we, us,** and **our,** which refer to Paul and those who were with him.*

1 THESSALONIANS 1:6-7

6 You also became imitators of us and of the Lord, having received the word in much tribulation with the joy of the Holy Spirit,

7 so that you became an example to all the believers in Macedonia and in Achaia.

1 THESSALONIANS 2:1-2,14

1 For you yourselves know, brethren, that our coming to you was not in vain,

2 but after we had already suffered and been mistreated in Philippi, as you know, we had the boldness in our God to speak to you the gospel of God amid much opposition.

14 For you, brethren, became imitators of the churches of God in Christ Jesus that are in Judea, for you also endured the same sufferings at the hands of your own countrymen, even as they did from the Jews....

1 THESSALONIANS 3:4

For indeed when we were with you, we kept telling you in advance that we were going to suffer affliction; and so it came to pass, as you know.

Leader: *Read aloud these same verses once more.*

- *This time have the group mark every reference to* **tribulation, suffered, mistreated,** *and* **affliction:**

DISCUSS

- What did you learn from making the references to the Thessalonian believers and Paul?

- Based on what you have seen to be true of their circumstances, what do you think the Thessalonians were examples of (1 Thessalonians 1:7)?

- How does this relate to what you learned in 2 Thessalonians 1?

- Based on what you've learned, how would you describe the believer's relationship with suffering?

- How does this relate to your life?

OBSERVE

Let's look at some other passages in which Paul spoke to believers about persecution and suffering.

Leader: *Read aloud Philippians 1:29-30 and 2 Timothy 3:12.*
- *Circle all references to the believer, including pronouns.*
- *Mark sufferings and persecution, as before:* /WV

granted; is a favor from
the Lord

PHILIPPIANS 1:29-30

29 For to you it has been granted for Christ's sake, not only to believe in Him, but also to suffer for His sake,

30 experiencing the same conflict which you saw in me, and now hear to be in me.

2 TIMOTHY 3:12

Indeed, all who desire to live godly in Christ Jesus will be persecuted.

INSIGHT

The word *granted* in Philippians 1:29 is translated from the Greek word *charizomai*, which means "to grant as a favor or to show kindness." It is the verb form of the noun for grace. Suffering is a privilege God gives to the believer, a form of grace that shows His favor toward us.

Paul wrote a second letter to Thessalonians

DISCUSS

• According to these verses, and the definition of the word *granted,* what conclusions can you draw regarding suffering and the believer?

• How does this relate to your present circumstances or to what you can expect as a believer?

2 THESSALONIANS 1:6-10

6 For after all it is only just for God to repay with affliction those who afflict you,

7 and to give relief to you who are afflicted and to us as well when the Lord Jesus will be revealed from heaven with His mighty angels in flaming fire,

OBSERVE

Let's return to 2 Thessalonians 1, where we began this week's study, and see what Paul told the Thessalonians about those who afflicted them.

Leader: *Read aloud 2 Thessalonians 1:6-10. Have the group…*

   • *draw a box around each phrase with the words **those** or **these,** which refer to people who afflict believers:* ☐

   • *mark every reference to **time** with a clock:* ⏰

DISCUSS

• What did you learn about those who afflict believers? What will happen to them and when will it happen?

They will have eternal life forever, whether heaven or well

• According to this passage, when will the believer be relieved from affliction?

• How do the truths you have just learned affect you?

Granded us strength privilege to soffer with the Lord.

• In the light of all you have studied this week, what have you learned about the role of suffering in the life of a believer? How will this impact your response to difficult circumstances?

Keep the faith, persevere Love grows when we pra in it together faith grows Don't surrender but endure in it God will repay those that afflict me. we can get up + move along

[8] dealing out retribution to those who do not know God and to those who do not obey the gospel of our Lord Jesus.

[9] These will pay the penalty of eternal destruction, away from the presence of the Lord and from the glory of His power,

[10] when He comes to be glorified in His saints on that day, and to be marveled at among all who have believed—for our testimony to you was believed.

WRAP IT UP

We often hear conflicting messages about suffering. Some of the popular teachings of the day indicate that once you have become a believer, your problems are resolved. Some preachers tell us that God intends for all His children to be wealthy and healthy. They claim that success, prosperity, and trouble-free living are yours for the taking—if you have enough faith or if you confess God's promises.

Is this teaching consistent with the Word of God? Is it consistent with what you have learned this week?

Like thousands of believers before us, we are living in difficult times. Christians all around us are under attack. When we stand up for God's truth, we find ourselves trampled by others marching under the banner of "tolerance." And we find that we're not immune to the pressures, suffering, and pain of daily life that threaten to crush us.

How will you respond to suffering? Will you spend your time complaining or perhaps even hide your faith? Will you try to escape persecution, or will you follow the example of the Thessalonians and persevere?

Last week we learned, through the lives of the believers in the early church, that suffering is a fact of life for all Christians, not just a chosen few. The Thessalonians suffered because they embraced the gospel, just as Paul suffered because he delivered the gospel to them.

We saw that the Thessalonians did not try to run from their difficulties; instead they trusted God and He enabled them to persevere. They were considered worthy of the kingdom of God because they endured their affliction with steadfast faith.

This week we will take a closer look at the life of Paul to gain a better understanding of why believers suffer and what forms that suffering may take.

OBSERVE

As we consider Paul's example, let's start with a passage where God spoke about Paul to a disciple named Ananias, just after the apostle-to-be encountered Christ on the road to Damascus.

Leader: Read aloud Acts 9:15-16.
  • *Have the group circle the pronouns* (**he**) *and* (**him**) *that refer to Paul.*

DISCUSS

• What was God's purpose for Paul's life?

ACTS 9:15-16

15 But the Lord said to him, "Go, for he is a chosen instrument of Mine, to bear My name before the Gentiles and kings and the sons of Israel;

16 for I will show him how much he must suffer for My name's sake."

• Why would Paul suffer?

OBSERVE

Keeping in mind what you've just learned, let's observe what happened on Paul's first missionary journey, when he was accompanied by Barnabas.

ACTS 13:44-45,49-50

44 The next Sabbath nearly the whole city assembled to hear the word of the Lord.

45 But when the Jews saw the crowds, they were filled with jealousy and began contradicting the things spoken by Paul, and were blaspheming.

49 And the word of the Lord was being spread through the whole region.

50 But the Jews incited the devout women of prominence and the leading men of the city, and instigated a persecution against

Leader: Read aloud Acts 13:44-45,49-50. Have the group…

• *draw a box around every reference to* ***the word of the Lord:*** ☐

• *put a* **J** *over each reference to the Jews.*

DISCUSS

• What did you learn from marking *the Word of the Lord*?

• How did the Jews respond to Paul's preaching of the Word of God?

• What insight do you gain from this incident in the lives of Paul and Barnabas about the possible consequences of proclaiming God's truth?

• Have you ever suffered for sharing the gospel? If so, describe your experience.

OBSERVE

Let's learn more about Paul's experience by reading a portion of his letter to Timothy, whose actions Paul contrasted with those of men who had opposed the truth.

Leader: *Read aloud 2 Timothy 3:10-12.*
  • *As you read, have the group mark* **persecution** *and* **sufferings,** *as before:*
  /MWV

DISCUSS

• What has been taking place in Paul's life?

• How did Timothy respond to Paul's example?

• What can you learn from Paul's example?

• How should Paul's experience impact your response to suffering?

Paul and Barnabas, and drove them out of their district.

2 TIMOTHY 3:10-12

10 Now you followed my teaching, conduct, purpose, faith, patience, love, perseverance,

11 persecution, and sufferings, such as happened to me at Antioch, at Iconium and at Lystra; what persecutions I endured, and out of them all the Lord rescued me!

12 Indeed, all who desire to live godly in Christ Jesus will be persecuted.

2 CORINTHIANS 1:8-9

8 For we do not want you to be unaware, brethren, of our affliction which came to us in Asia, that we were burdened excessively, beyond our strength, so that we despaired even of life;

9 indeed, we had the sentence of death within ourselves so that we would not trust in ourselves, but in God who raises the dead.

OBSERVE

In this next passage Paul is speaking to the Corinthian believers about things he and Timothy had experienced.

Leader: Read aloud 2 Corinthians 1:8-9 and have the group...
- *mark **affliction** as before:* 𝓜𝓦𝓥
- *circle the plural pronouns **we, our, us,** and **ourselves.***

DISCUSS

- Describe how Paul and Timothy were affected by the affliction that came upon them.

- What was the purpose of this suffering? (Note the phrase "so that" in verse 9.)

- Describe a situation in which you were burdened excessively, beyond your strength. How did you respond?

INSIGHT

We learned last week that the Greek word for *affliction* is *thlipsis,* which means "to crush or to squeeze." The word usually refers to suffering from outward circumstances. Affliction could be anything that burdens the spirit. In 2 Corinthians 1:8, Paul indicated a burden that was excessive and beyond his ability to endure.

• Now just to make sure you don't miss the point, according to what Paul wrote to the Corinthians, what do situations like this teach us?

Trust v God not self
Gods in control...

James 1 - 21-24
Hebrews - CLS

OBSERVE

Leader: *Read aloud what Paul says to the believers in 2 Corinthians 4:7-11. Have the group...*

- *circle each occurrence of **we** and **ourselves.***
- *draw a slash (/) between phrases in which Paul shows **a contrast.** These contrasts are usually indicated by the word "but."*

---

2 CORINTHIANS 4:7-11

7 But we have this treasure in earthen vessels, so that the surpassing greatness of the power will be of God and not from ourselves;

8 we are afflicted in every way, but not crushed; perplexed, but not despairing;

9 persecuted but not forsaken; struck down, but not destroyed;

10 always carrying about in the body the dying of Jesus, so that the life of Jesus also may be manifested in our body.

11 For we who live are constantly being delivered over to death for Jesus' sake, so that the life of Jesus also may be manifested in our mortal flesh.

INSIGHT

The *treasure* referred to in verse 7 is a spiritual treasure relating to eternal life, the gospel message. The phrase *earthen vessels* refers to the human body, which is the container that holds the treasure. The body is weak in contrast to the greatness of power found in God.

DISCUSS

• What did you learn from marking references to Paul and his fellow believers in these verses?

• What did the contrasts reveal about their response to difficult circumstances?

we have great ness, victory)

• Why were they suffering? According to verses 10 and 11, what would be accomplished through their affliction?

Dying of Jesus. so he don be manifested in us

• What was God's role in all this?

God kept him strong) He delivered over dan

OBSERVE

Leader: Read aloud 2 Corinthians 11:30 and 2 Corinthians 12:9-10.

- *Have the group draw a box* ☐ *around the pronouns **I, me,** and **my,** which refer to Paul.*

Leader: Read aloud these same verses once more and have the group do the following:

- *Draw a squiggly line under the references to **weak** or **weakness:** 〰️*
- *Draw a cloud shape like this ☁ around references to **power** or **strength.***

DISCUSS

- What did you learn from marking the references to Paul? What did he choose to boast about?

- What was Paul's attitude regarding weakness and why?

  Praise the Lord

- Why could Paul respond to his circumstances in this manner?

- What is your attitude toward weakness?

2 CORINTHIANS 11:30

If I have to boast, I will boast of what pertains to my weakness.

2 CORINTHIANS 12:9-10

9 And He has said to me, "My grace is sufficient for you, for power is perfected in weakness." Most gladly, therefore, I will rather boast about my weaknesses, so that the power of Christ may dwell in me.

10 Therefore I am well content with weaknesses, with insults, with distresses, with persecutions, with difficulties, for Christ's sake; for when I am weak, then I am strong.

- How does this compare with the world's view of weakness?

INSIGHT

The Greek word *charis*, translated in this passage as *grace*, means "graciousness, unearned merit or favor."

We are saved by grace, according to (Ephesians 2:8-9.) We also live by grace. God divinely enables us with a strength that is continually sufficient to overcome our weaknesses. In His grace we receive the power to do what we cannot do ourselves. But first we must recognize our weakness, submit ourselves to God, and put our trust in Him.

- How does this insight regarding grace relate to your life and to your circumstances?

OBSERVE

Let's read more about Paul's response to suffering.

Leader: Read aloud 2 Corinthians 7:5-7. Have the group...

- *mark each reference to **affliction** or **afflicted**: ⋀⋁*
- *mark each reference to **comfort** with a* **C.**

DISCUSS

- Describe Paul's afflictions.

- In what ways can you relate to his experience?

- How was Paul comforted?

- Where do you find comfort in the midst of suffering or affliction?

OBSERVE

We've seen how Paul found strength and comfort in the midst of his suffering. In the following passage, we read more of his perspective on difficult circumstances.

2 CORINTHIANS 7:5-7

5 For even when we came into Macedonia our flesh had no rest, but we were afflicted on every side: conflicts without, fears within.

6 But God, who comforts the depressed, comforted us by the coming of Titus;

7 and not only by his coming, but also by the comfort with which he was comforted in you, as he reported to us your longing, your mourning, your zeal for me; so that I rejoiced even more.

PHILIPPIANS 1:12-14

12 Now I want you to know, brethren, that my circumstances have turned out for the

greater progress of the gospel,

13 so that my imprisonment in the cause of Christ has become well known throughout the whole praetorian guard and to everyone else,

14 and that most of the brethren, trusting in the Lord because of my imprisonment, have far more courage to speak the word of God without fear.

ROMANS 8:35-39

35 Who will separate us from the love of Christ? Will tribulation, or distress, or persecution, or famine, or nakedness, or peril, or sword?

Leader: Read aloud Philippians 1:12-14.

> • *As you read, have the group draw a box around each reference to **Paul,** including pronouns.*

DISCUSS

• What did you learn about Paul? What were his circumstances?

• How did Paul view his circumstances?

• If you were imprisoned—literally or figuratively—by suffering or affliction for the cause of Christ, what would your attitude, your focus be?

• If others followed your example, what impact would it have on them? on those around them?

OBSERVE

Paul didn't merely survive his sufferings; he lived victoriously in the midst of difficult circumstances.

Leader: Read Romans 8:35-39 aloud. Have the group...

- *draw a box around the pronouns **I, we,** and **us,** which refer to Paul and his fellow believers:* ⬚

- *mark each reference to love with a heart:* ♡

DISCUSS

- What did you learn from marking the pronouns *I, we,* and *us*?

- To whom do these truths apply?

- As followers of Christ, what should we focus on when tribulations, persecutions, and afflictions overwhelm us?

- Have you ever doubted God's love in the midst of your suffering? What did you learn from marking *love* in this passage? How does this affect your view of suffering and of God?

- How convinced was Paul of God's love? And how convinced are you?

36 Just as it is written, "For Your sake we are being put to death all day long; we were considered as sheep to be slaughtered."

37 But in all these things we overwhelmingly conquer through Him who loved us.

38 For I am convinced that neither death, nor life, nor angels, nor principalities, nor things present, nor things to come, nor powers,

39 nor height, nor depth, nor any other created thing, will be able to separate us from the love of God, which is in Christ Jesus our Lord.

WRAP IT UP

Paul, the chief persecutor of the early church, became one of the persecuted for his belief in Jesus Christ. After Paul met Jesus Christ on the road to Damascus, God called him to bear the name of Jesus to the Gentiles, warning him that he would suffer for His name's sake. Yet, Paul never stopped preaching the Word of God. Regardless of the cost, Paul persevered.

His life reveals what it means to live victoriously in the midst of trials and suffering. He was excessively burdened beyond his strength, yet he did not trust in himself; he trusted in God. He was afflicted with outward conflicts and inward fears, yet he was comforted by God and by others. He recognized that he was a humanly weak vessel whose power was from God and not from within himself. Paul showed us that nothing can separate us from the love of Christ, and he revealed to us the key to victory: We overwhelmingly conquer through Jesus Christ.

Have you ever been overwhelmed by the challenges and difficulties of life? How do you respond when you have to deal with conflicts and fears? Are you following Paul's example?

What will you do with the truths you have learned this week? When conflicts arise, when relationships are strained because of life's pressures, how will you respond? Will you run the other way? Will you take matters into your own hands and try to solve your problems? Or will you trust in the Lord to be your strength?

As we focused on Paul in our last lesson, we learned about the sufferings and persecutions he encountered. We observed his trust in the all-sufficient grace of God to enable him to persevere. Paul was steadfast in his faith; he did not retreat or back down from the mission God had given him. So why did God allow this faithful servant to suffer? And why does He permit pain in our lives?

OBSERVE

We will begin our study this week by evaluating what Jesus told His disciples about the role of suffering in their lives.

Leader: *Read aloud John 15:18-21.*
  • *Have the group circle the pronouns* **you** *and* **yours,** *which refer to the disciples of Jesus:* ◯

Remember to have the students say aloud the word they are marking so they can be sure to note each reference.

Leader: *Read aloud John 15:18-21 again and have the group…*
  • *mark each occurrence of* **hate** *or* **hated** *like this:* ♡
  • *mark each reference to* **persecute:** /W/

JOHN 15:18-21

18 "If the world hates you, you know that it has hated Me before it hated you.

19 "If you were of the world, the world would love its own; but because you are not of the world, but I chose you out of the world, because of this the world hates you.

20 "Remember the word that I said to you, 'A slave is not greater than his master.' If they

persecuted Me, they
will also persecute you;
if they kept My word,
they will keep yours
also.

21 "But all these
things they will do to
you for My name's
sake, because they do
not know the One
who sent Me."

1 PETER 2:18-21

18 Servants, be sub-
missive to your mas-
ters with all respect,
not only to those who
are good and gentle,
but also to those who
are unreasonable.

19 For this finds
favor, if for the sake of
conscience toward
God a person bears up

DISCUSS

• What did you learn about the disciples
and Jesus when you marked *hate* and
persecute? We're going to be
hated & persecuted for
being a follower

• According to these verses, why do believers suffer? Because I'm a child
of God

• How does this relate to you? Have you
ever experienced hatred or persecution
because of your relationship with Christ?
Lost a job

• What specific truths in this passage will
help you endure hatred or persecution?

OBSERVE

Leader: *Read aloud 1 Peter 2:18-21. Have
the group...*

> • *circle the pronouns* **you** *and* **your,**
> *which refer to the believer:*
> • *mark every reference to* **suffering** *as
> before:*

Leader: *Read aloud 1 Peter 2:18-21 again.*

> • *Draw a box around each occurrence of*
> **this finds favor.**

DISCUSS

• In what way are servants instructed to respond to their masters?

Be Submissive

• What did you learn from marking *suffering*? What reason is given in this passage for the suffering of believers?

To learn to endure with patience.

• What finds favor with God?

Patiently enduring the harsh treatment

• According to verse 21, for what purpose have believers been called?

for his purpose

OBSERVE

Leader: *Read aloud 1 Peter 2:21-24.*

• *Have the group mark each reference to* **Christ,** *including the pronouns, with a cross:* †

under sorrows when suffering unjustly.

20 For what credit is there if, when you sin and are harshly treated, you endure it with patience? But if when you do what is right and suffer for it you patiently endure it, this finds favor with God.

21 For you have been called for this purpose, since Christ also suffered for you, leaving you an example for you to follow in His steps.

1 PETER 2:21-24

21 For you have been called for this purpose, since Christ also suffered for you, leaving you an example for you to follow in His steps, †

22 who committed no sin, nor was any deceit found in His mouth;

23 and while being reviled, He did not revile in return; while suffering, He uttered no threats, but kept entrusting Himself to Him who judges right-eously;

24 and He Himself bore our sins in His body on the cross, so that we might die to sin and live to right-eousness; for by His wounds you were healed.

DISCUSS

• Look at each place you marked *Jesus* and note what you observed about His example in suffering. Discuss the specific actions Jesus took or chose not to take in response to suffering.

He entrusted Himself to Him who judges righteously

• In what ways do people usually respond when they are treated harshly or unjustly?

Lash out

INSIGHT
Revile means "to verbally abuse."

• Based on what you observed from the response of Jesus when He suffered, what specific things should you do or not do when faced with suffering?

• How does your life align with Christ's example? When others see you suffering, what similarities or differences do they notice between you and Jesus?

OBSERVE

Leader: Read aloud Hebrews 5:8.

- *Have the group mark each reference to*
  Christ, *including the pronouns, with a*
  cross: †

Although He was a Son, He learned obedience from the things which He suffered.

DISCUSS

- What did you learn about Jesus in this passage?

- What does this verse indicate we can learn from our own suffering?

OBSERVE

We've observed Christ's response to suffering. Now let's look at some specific ways His example can guide our own response to trials.

Leader: Read aloud 1 Peter 4:1-2, 14-16, 19. Have your students…

- *mark **suffering** as before:* ⋀⋀⋁
- *underline **the instructions** given to believers in this passage.*

1 PETER 4:1-2,14-16,19

¹ Therefore, since Christ has suffered in the flesh, arm yourselves also with the same purpose, because he who has suffered in the flesh has ceased from sin,

² so as to live the rest of the time in the flesh no longer for the lusts of men, but for the will of God.

14 If you are reviled *verbally Abuse* for the name of Christ, you are blessed, because the Spirit of glory and of God rests on you.

15 Make sure that none of you suffers as a murderer, or thief, or evildoer, or a troublesome meddler;

16 but if anyone suffers as a Christian, he is not to be ashamed, but is to glorify God in this name.

19 Therefore, those also who suffer according to the will of God shall entrust their souls to a faithful Creator in doing what is right.

1 PETER 3:14-17

14 But even if you should suffer for the sake of righteousness, you are blessed. And

DISCUSS

• What did you learn from marking *suffering*? What are some reasons a person might suffer?

• What are you instructed to do when you suffer? Why?

rely on God completely

OBSERVE

Leader: *Read aloud 1 Peter 3:14-17. Have the group…*

- *mark **righteousness** with an **R**.*
- *draw a box around the word **blessed:***

Leader: *Read these verses aloud again. Have the group…*

- *mark* **suffering** *and* **persecution** *as before:* /MW/
- *underline* **the instructions** *given to believers in this passage, those things we are to do and not to do.*

DISCUSS

- Look at the places where you marked references to suffering and persecution and discuss the reasons for that suffering.

- What benefit or result comes from suffering?

INSIGHT

The Greek word translated in this passage as *blessed* is *makarios*. It means "to be satisfied fully." This satisfaction comes from God; it does not depend on circumstances.

---

do not fear their intimidation, and do not be troubled,

15 but sanctify Christ as Lord in your hearts, always being ready to make a defense to everyone who asks you to give an account for the hope that is in you, yet with gentleness and reverence;

16 and keep a good conscience so that in the thing in which you are slandered, those who revile your good behavior in Christ will be put to shame.

17 For it is better, if God should will it so, that you suffer for doing what is right rather than for doing what is wrong.

- Look at the instructions you have underlined. What are you to do when you suffer? What are some ways you are not to respond?

- Consider a recent—or current—circumstance in your life that involved suffering. Was your response in line with the instructions of Scripture? In what ways will you change your response to trials in the future?

MATTHEW 5:11-12

11 "Blessed are you when people insult you and persecute you, and falsely say all kinds of evil against you because of Me.

12 "Rejoice and be glad, for your reward in heaven is great; for in the same way they persecuted the prophets who were before you."

OBSERVE

Let's look at a passage where Jesus advised His followers about how to conduct their lives if they wanted to inherit the kingdom of God.

Leader: *Read aloud Matthew 5:11-12. Have the group say aloud and…*
- *mark each reference to **persecute:** /W/*
- *underline **the instructions** Jesus gave to His followers.*

DISCUSS

• According to these verses, in what ways can followers of Jesus expect to suffer?

• How are they to respond?

• What encouragement did you find in this passage? What promises do you see?

OBSERVE

Leader: Read aloud Romans 8:18.
> • *Have the group mark **suffering** as before.*

DISCUSS

• What did you learn about suffering?

• How could this truth be applied when you are dealing with the pain in your own life?

OBSERVE

Leader: Read aloud 1 Peter 4:12-14. Have the group...

ROMANS 8:18

For I consider that the sufferings of this present time are not worthy to be compared with the glory that is to be revealed to us.

Amen!

1 PETER 4:12-14

12 Beloved, do not be surprised at the fiery ordeal among you, which comes upon you for your testing, as though some strange thing were happening to you;

13 but to the degree that you share the sufferings of Christ, keep on rejoicing, so that also at the revelation of His glory you may rejoice with exultation.

14 If you are reviled for the name of Christ, you are blessed, because the Spirit of glory and of God rests on you.

- *circle the pronouns **you** and **your**, which refer to the believer.*

- *underline **the instructions** given to believers in this passage, those things we are to do and not to do.*

INSIGHT

The word *fiery* in verse 12 is translated from the Greek word *purosis.* In this passage it refers to burning, the process used for refining or purifying metals, as well as to trials or calamities that test or purify the character of a person.

In the same verse the word *testing* is translated from the Greek word *peirasmo.* In this context, the testing is sent by God or allowed by God and indicates trying one's character to prove him or her faithful.

DISCUSS

- What is the believer instructed to do?

- Keeping in mind the definitions you have just learned, what can you conclude about suffering?

• What have you learned about the personal benefit of suffering?

OBSERVE

Leader: Read aloud Psalm 66:8-12.

• *Have the group mark each reference to* **God,** *including the pronouns* **You, His, I,** *and* **My,** *with a triangle:* △

DISCUSS

• What did you learn about God from these verses? What had He done to and for His people?

• How does this relate to what you just learned in 1 Peter 4:12-14?

• What is the final outcome of this refining process?

• Share some ways that God has tested you. What were the results? Based on what you've learned this week, how might you respond to a similar testing in the future?

PSALM 66:8-12

8 Bless our God, O peoples, and sound His praise abroad,

9 who keeps us in life and does not allow our feet to slip.

10 For You have tried us, O God; You have refined us as silver is refined.

11 You brought us into the net; You laid an oppressive burden upon our loins.

12 You made men ride over our heads; we went through fire and through water, yet You brought us out into a place of abundance.

WRAP IT UP

Consider for a moment the ancient process used to refine and purify metals: The silversmith would heat the silver ore in a clay crucible. He would control the temperature of the fire by using bellows and never left the fire unattended.

As the silver was heated, the impurities would rise to the top and the silversmith would skim them off the surface. This process was repeated until all of the impurities were removed. The silversmith knew the process was complete when he could see his image reflected in the silver.

So, too, God refines His precious children through a similar process. Like a silversmith, He casts His people into the furnace of affliction, the refiner's fire. He controls the intensity of the trial, knowing just how much heat is needed to bring our impurities to the surface. He never leaves us nor forsakes us. He stays with us throughout the refining process. His ultimate purpose is to refine and purify us so that we will reflect His image.

When you are in the midst of a trial, what are you reflecting to those around you? Can others see the Lord and His character mirrored in your life? Does your response honor Him and demonstrate your faith?

WEEK FOUR

In our study over the past few weeks, we have observed the example of Paul, who was excessively burdened beyond his strength, afflicted on every side by conflicts from without and fears from within. Yet Paul chose to trust in God and not in himself.

We also have seen that Christ's response to suffering gave us an example to follow. He never acted independently of God, but entrusted Himself to God who judges righteously.

Our study has confirmed that, as believers, we will suffer for our faith. We may even be persecuted for doing what is right. Though it may be difficult to understand, these trials are a gift from our gracious God, who uses suffering to purify us and prove us faithful so that we will reflect who He is to others. Our response to trials and difficulties should bring honor and glory to the Lord.

This week we'll discover how living out these truths impacts the life of a believer. We will begin by looking at the example of Job, who endured trials few of us can even imagine.

OBSERVE

Leader: *Read aloud Job 1:6-12. As you read have the group do the following:*

- *Mark **God,** and the pronouns and synonyms that refer to Him, with a triangle:* △
- *Draw a pitchfork over every reference to **Satan,** like this:* ⚁

JOB 1:6-12

6 Now there was a day when the sons of God came to present themselves before the LORD, and Satan also came among them.

7 The LORD said to Satan, "From where do

you come?" Then Satan answered the LORD and said, "From roaming about on the earth and walking around on it."

⁸ The LORD said to Satan, "Have you considered My servant Job? For there is no one like him on the earth, a blameless and upright man, fearing God and turning away from evil."

⁹ Then Satan answered the LORD, "Does Job fear God for nothing?

¹⁰ "Have You not made a hedge about him and his house and all that he has, on every side? You have blessed the work of his hands, and his possessions have increased in the land.

Leader: *Read aloud Job 1:6-12 a second time.*

  • *Circle **Job** and the pronouns that refer to him:* ⬭

DISCUSS
• Briefly summarize what is happening in this passage.

• Beginning at verse 6, what did you learn from marking the references to Satan?

• How did God describe Job? What did you learn about Job's relationship with God?

• What question does Satan raise regarding Job's motive for serving and fearing God? According to Satan, how would Job respond to suffering?

• What resulted from the meeting between the Lord and Satan?

• Who initiated the testing of Job?

OBSERVE

Leader: *Read aloud 1 Peter 5:8.*

> • *Have the group mark **the devil** and **adversary** with a pitchfork:*

DISCUSS

• What did you learn about the devil? What is his motive? What opportunity is he seeking?

11 "But put forth Your hand now and touch all that he has; he will surely curse You to Your face."

12 Then the LORD said to Satan, "Behold, all that he has is in your power, only do not put forth your hand on him." So Satan departed from the presence of the LORD.

1 PETER 5:8

Be of sober spirit, be on the alert. Your adversary, the devil, prowls around like a roaring lion, seeking someone to devour.

• How does this relate to what you learned in Job 1:6-12?

JOB 1:20-22

20 Then Job arose and tore his robe and shaved his head, and he fell to the ground and worshiped.

21 He said, "Naked I came from my mother's womb, and naked I shall return there. The LORD gave and the LORD has taken away. Blessed be the name of the LORD."

22 Through all this Job did not sin nor did he blame God.

OBSERVE

As a result of God's conversations with Satan about Job, everything was taken from him—his children, his servants, his livestock, his health, and his fortune.

Leader: Read aloud Job 1:20-22. As you read have the group say aloud and...
  • *circle every reference to **Job.***

DISCUSS

• What did you learn about Job's response to his difficult circumstances?

• What does this tell you about Job's relationship with God?

Job suffered because of his heart

OBSERVE

Leader: Read aloud Job 6:10; 42:10; and James 5:11. As you read have the group...

- *circle each reference to **Job**.*
- *mark each reference to **the Lord** with a triangle:* △

DISCUSS

- How did Job respond to suffering?

JOB 6:10

But it is still my consolation, and I rejoice in unsparing pain, that I have not denied the words of the Holy One.

JOB 42:10

The LORD restored the fortunes of Job when he prayed for his friends, and the LORD increased all that Job had twofold.

JAMES 5:11

We count those blessed who endured. You have heard of the endurance of Job and have seen the outcome of the Lord's dealings, that the Lord is full of compassion and is merciful.

- What did the Lord do for Job and how did He deal with him?

- As a result of what you have learned thus far in this lesson, who or what was the source of Job's suffering?

- Was Job's suffering brought on by sin in his life?

- Review the first paragraph under "Observe" on page 40 and think about the specific losses Job experienced. Have you experienced any of these losses in your own life? If so, what questions did you wrestle with? How did you respond to your suffering?

OBSERVE

Leader: Read aloud James 1:2-4. Have the group...

- *circle the words that refer to* **the believer,** *including* **brethren, you,** *and* **your.**
- *mark* **trials** *and* **testing** *like this:* /w\

DISCUSS

- What is the believer specifically instructed to do? What knowledge enables the believer to respond in this way?

INSIGHT

The Greek word translated as *perfect* in this passage means "mature, developed fully." It does not imply perfection but indicates that you have attained your intended goal.

Complete means "whole, having all its parts."

JAMES 1:2-4

2 Consider it all joy, my brethren, when you encounter various trials,

3 knowing that the testing of your faith produces endurance.

4 And let endurance have its perfect result, so that you may be perfect and complete, lacking in nothing.

Instruction

God's Strength & Joy!

• According to what you read in James, how is endurance developed in the life of the believer?

• What does endurance bring about?

1 PETER 1:6-7

6 In this you greatly rejoice, even though now for a little while, if necessary, you have been distressed by various trials,

7 so that the proof of your faith, being more precious than gold which is perishable, even though tested by fire, may be found to result in praise and glory and honor at the revelation of Jesus Christ.

OBSERVE

Leader: *Read aloud 1 Peter 1:6-7. Have the group…*
- *circle the pronouns that refer to **the believer.***
- *mark **trials** and **tested** as before.*

DISCUSS

• What did you learn about the purpose of trials in the life of the believer?

• What did you learn about the relationship between trials and faith?

• How did the truths of this lesson impact your understanding of the adversities and difficulties you experience?

OBSERVE

In Romans 1–4, the apostle Paul established that all are sinners and need salvation. He also made clear that salvation is found only through faith in Jesus Christ. In light of these truths, Romans 5:1 opens with the term "therefore," indicating the result for those who have been justified or declared righteous by their faith.

Leader: Read aloud Romans 5:1-5. Have the group say aloud and...
  • *circle the pronouns that refer to **the believer,** including **we, our,** and **us.***

Leader: Read aloud Romans 5:1-5 once more to be sure you grasp its meaning.

ROMANS 5:1-5

¹ Therefore, having been justified by faith, we have peace with God through our Lord Jesus Christ,

² through whom also we have obtained our introduction by faith into this grace in which we stand; and we exult in hope of the glory of God.

³ And not only this, but we also exult in our tribulations,

knowing that tribulation brings about perseverance;

4 and perseverance, proven character; and proven character, hope;

5 and hope does not disappoint, because the love of God has been poured out within our hearts through the Holy Spirit who was given to us.

DISCUSS

• According to these verses, what does every believer have as a result of being justified?

• What is every believer to do and why?

INSIGHT

Exult means "to boast in regard to anything."

In Romans 5:3 the preposition *in* may seem like a small, insignificant word, but it is key to understanding the full impact of this passage. It is translated from the Greek word *en,* which means "remaining in place or resting in." Rather than moving into or out of the situation, it indicates a total lack of motion. In other words, one is at rest, not attempting to get out of the tribulation.

The Greek word translated as *brings about* is *katergazomai,* which means "to carry out a task until it is finished." In the context of this passage in Romans, the phrase indicates completing a task, the result of which is to bring out something that is already present. Tribulation in the life of the believer brings out perseverance, because the grace to persevere comes from the inner strength God has given us.

• What should you do when you find yourself in a difficult situation? Why?

JAMES 1:5-8

5 But if any of you lacks wisdom, let him ask of God, who gives to all generously and without reproach, and it will be given to him.

6 But he must ask in faith without any doubting, for the one who doubts is like the surf of the sea, driven and tossed by the wind.

7 For that man ought not to expect that he will receive anything from the Lord,

8 being a double-minded man, unstable in all his ways.

OBSERVE

Now let's return to James 1, which tells us what to do when we don't know how to handle our difficult circumstances.

Leader: Read aloud James 1:5-8.
  • *Have the group underline **the instructions** given to believers in this passage.*

INSIGHT

The Greek word for *wisdom* is *Sophia,* which means "divine wisdom." *Wisdom* refers to the ability of the believer to apply God's perspective to issues in his or her life.

DISCUSS

• According to these verses, what are we as believers to do when we find ourselves in difficult situations?

Recive a crown of life if we hang through

• How does God promise to help in difficult situations?

• What are the conditions we must meet to claim this promise?

Refine me by fire. Pray. Ask God. Be without Doubt

OBSERVE

Leader: *Read aloud 1 Corinthians 10:13. Have the group...*
- *mark the references to **temptation** and **tempted** with a **T**.*
- *circle the pronoun **you,** which refers to **the believer.***

1 CORINTHIANS 10:13

No temptation has overtaken you but such as is common to man; and God is faithful, who will not allow you to be tempted beyond what you are able, but with the temptation will provide the way of escape also, so that you will be able to endure it.

INSIGHT

The Greek word for *temptation* is the same word, *peirasmos,* which was used in James 1:2. This word can be translated as "temptation, trial, or testing."

Temptation itself is not sinful. Rather, it is how we choose to respond to the temptation that determines the outcome. The temptation is a test of whether we will choose to walk in obedience to God or disobey and sin.

DISCUSS

• What did you learn from this verse about the believer and temptation?

• What choice does a person have when faced with temptation?

• How does knowing this prepare you to respond when you are tempted to do wrong or when you are in a trial?

HEBREWS 2:18

For since He Himself was tempted in that which He has suffered, He is able to come to the aid of those who are tempted.

HEBREWS 4:15

For we do not have a high priest who cannot sympathize with our weaknesses, but One who has been tempted in all things as we are, yet without sin.

OBSERVE

We've seen that God sends temptation and trials as tests of our faith, part of the refining process to make us more like Christ. Let's look more closely at Jesus, who not only serves as our example but also as our Intercessor and High Priest.

Leader: Read aloud Hebrews 2:18 and Hebrews 4:15. Have the group...
   • mark the references to **Jesus,** including pronouns, with a cross: †
   • mark a T over each occurrence of **tempted.**

Bind in Jesus Name

DISCUSS

• What did you learn from marking the references to Jesus?

The Lord understands and he forgives

• What is true for the believer? What help do you find in these verses for dealing with temptation?

Feed yourself with the word

Romans 12:2

OBSERVE

Leader: *Read aloud Hebrews 12:1-3. As you read, have the group…*

> • *circle the pronouns* **we, us, our, and you,** *which refer to* **the believer:** ◯
> • *mark* **Jesus** *and the pronouns that refer to Him with a cross, as before:* ✝

Leader: *Read aloud Hebrews 12:1-3 once more.*

> • *Have the group underline* **the instructions** *given to believers in this passage.*

HEBREWS 12:1-3

1 Therefore, since we have so great a cloud of witnesses surrounding us, let us also lay aside every encumbrance and the sin which so easily entangles us, and let us run with endurance the race that is set before us,

2 fixing our eyes on Jesus, the author and perfecter of faith, who

for the joy set before Him endured the cross, despising the shame, and has sat down at the right hand of the throne of God.

3 For consider Him who has endured such hostility by sinners against Himself, so that you will not grow weary and lose heart.

INSIGHT

The Greek word for *race* is *agon*, from which we get our word *agony*. The race of faith can be agonizing. It demands discipline and perseverance. Following Christ is not a fifty-yard dash but a marathon—and it demands our all.

DISCUSS

• According to this passage, what is the believer instructed to do? Why?

• How does the believer prepare to do this?

• What did you learn about Jesus and His response to hostility? What encouragement does His example offer?

INSIGHT

An encumbrance is something that hinders you or weighs you down.

• What are some of the encumbrances, snares, or hindrances that trip you up in the race of faith?

Lay burdens aside over x over !!!

Speed is not everything, direction counts. slow down

WRAP IT UP

Like Job, you may experience suffering even when you fear God and live uprightly and blamelessly before Him. You have faithful examples to follow. You have the assurance through the life of Jesus Christ and through others who have gone before you that you will be able to endure.

Testing in our lives produces endurance, just as it did in the life of Job. In Job's case God initiated the trial with Satan, but in His sovereignty and His omniscience, He knew what the outcome would be. In the midst of his heartache and pain, Job continued to praise and worship God. When others might have blamed God or turned on Him in anger, Job did not sin but remained faithful. Job passed the test, and God blessed the latter days of Job more than He did in the beginning.

Jesus did not sin when He was tempted. He entrusted Himself to the Father when He experienced tremendous trials. He can sympathize with our weaknesses and our temptations because He has been through it all Himself.

We may not always understand why we have to go through the trials and difficulties, but we can rest in the fact that God understands and promises we will never be given more than we can bear. We can be certain He is working out His purpose in our lives and using our experiences for the benefit of others.

As you face the challenges of living the Christian life and dealing with trials and difficulties…

- will you fix your eyes on Jesus, the author and perfecter of our faith?
- will you lay aside every obstacle that would keep you from finishing the race?
- will you run the race with endurance without growing weary and losing heart?
- will you be an example to others of the truths you have learned this week?

why do you serve God? (Job 38, 39, 40, 41)

my eyes are open!
The Lord is worthy!
Job's wife said curse God + die!
She saw his dispair and her loss,

Job needed to Humble Himself

Christ is a game changer

Have you ever felt totally overwhelmed because of circumstances over which you had no control? Perhaps you wondered whether the pain would ever stop and if your troubled heart would ever again find peace.

Where can you turn in these times of trouble?

God desires for us to come to Him in our pain—to know Him, to trust Him, and to know His Word—so that we can live victoriously in the midst of even the most challenging circumstances.

pray for friends

Gods word is Life

Always adjust your walk w/ the Lord

OBSERVE

Let's begin this week's study by reading the reassurance Jesus offered to His disciples in the upper room the night before He was crucified.

Leader: *Read aloud John 14:1.*

• *Have the group say aloud and underline* **Jesus' instructions to His disciples.**

JOHN 14:1

Do not let your heart be troubled; believe in God, believe also in Me.

Skill

Mocked God? Do I get upset or do I just go along?

DISCUSS

• What were the disciples instructed to do? And what were they not to do?

A home is not an address! What is Home to you?

INSIGHT

Troubled in this verse is translated from the Greek word *tarasso*. It means "to take away calmness of mind." It implies an action that strikes a person's spirit with fear and doubt.

    Believe is translated from the Greek word *pisteuo*. It means "to be persuaded of, to place confidence in, to trust, to rely upon."

• How do these definitions expand your understanding of this verse?

OBSERVE

According to what we just read, we are not supposed to have troubled hearts, nor are we to be filled with fear and doubt. We're instructed to keep our minds and hearts clear and calm, trusting in God and in His Son. What do we need to know about God in order to accomplish this?

God can do anything, he's my safe place.

use the word trouble to not rest.

Run to God's Arms for security

Leader: *Read aloud Psalm 37:39-40 and Isaiah 26:3-4. As you read, have the group…*

- *mark **the Lord** and the pronouns that refer to Him with a triangle:* △
- *underline **the instructions** given to the person facing trouble.*

Trust him completely and OBEY

DISCUSS

- Evaluate each reference to the Lord. What did you learn about Him and His response to those in trouble?

- What action is the person facing trouble instructed to take?

- What truths in these verses will help you place your confidence in God when trouble comes?

OBSERVE

Leader: *Read aloud Proverbs 18:10 and Psalm 20:1,5, and 7. Have the group do the following:*

PSALM 37:39-40

39 But the salvation *David* of the righteous is from the LORD; He is their strength in time of trouble.

40 The LORD helps them and delivers them; He delivers them from the wicked and saves them, because they take refuge in Him.

ISAIAH 26:3-4

3 The steadfast of mind You will keep in perfect peace, because he trusts in You.

4 Trust in the LORD forever, for in God the LORD, we have an everlasting Rock.

Banners have meaning: Declaring what I stand for

PROVERBS 18:10

The name of the LORD
is a strong tower; the
righteous runs into it
and is safe.

- *Draw a cloud shape like this* ☁
  around **name of the Lord** *and* **name
  of God.**
- *Underline* **the action(s)** *that the righteous person should take.*

PSALM 20:1,5,7

David

¹ May the LORD
answer you in the day
of trouble! May the
name of the God of
Jacob set you securely
on high!

⁵ We will sing for
joy over your victory,
and in the name of
our God we will set up
our banners. May the
LORD fulfill all your
petitions.

⁷ Some boast in
chariots and some in
horses, but we will
boast in the name of
the LORD, our God.

INSIGHT

The word *banner* in Psalm 20:5 is
translated from the Hebrew word
dagal. It means "to raise a flag or a
standard." A banner was carried at
the head of a military body and
served as a rallying point for the
army. In the Old Testament, banners
identified each of the tribes of Israel.
In Exodus 17 when the Israelites battled the Amalekites, Moses held up
the staff of God. As long as he held
the staff high, the Israelites prevailed. After their victory, Moses built
an altar, which he called "The LORD
is My Banner," or Jehovah-Nissi. The
same is true for us today: When we
run to God, as the Lord our banner,
in His strength we will find victory in
our difficulties.

Boost means glory;
Debbie Frysinger

DISCUSS

• What did you learn about the name of the Lord?

• What action is the righteous person to take?

INSIGHT

The first mention of *boast* in Psalm 20:7 can also be translated as *to trust*. The second mention of *boast* means "to call to mind, to remember." Remembering could also involve a public proclaiming of what is being remembered—in this case, the name of the Lord.

• What insights do you find in these verses for dealing with trials in your life?

PSALM 20:7

Some boast in chariots and some in horses, but we will boast in the name of the LORD, our God.

JEREMIAH 9:23-24

23 Thus says the LORD, "Let not a wise man boast of his wisdom, and let not the mighty man boast of his might, let not a rich man boast of his riches;

24 but let him who boasts boast of this, that he understands and knows Me, that I am the LORD who exercises lovingkindness, justice and righteousness on earth; for I delight in these things," declares the LORD.

OBSERVE

Leader: Read aloud Psalm 20:7 and Jeremiah 9:23-24.

> • *Have the group underline each occurrence of **boast**.*

INSIGHT

The word *boast* in the context of these passages means "to praise, to glory, or to brag about."

DISCUSS

• What did you learn from marking the word *boast*?

• Think about your conversations during the past week or so. Who or what has been the subject of your boasting?

• What should you boast in? Why?

• How does this kind of boasting fit with the world we live in? What do people generally boast about?

OBSERVE

We have just learned that we are to boast in, or to glory in, the name of the Lord. But we also are to glory in understanding and knowing God.

Leader: *Read aloud Psalm 46:10 and Daniel 11:32b.*

- *Have the group draw a box around each occurrence of the word **know**:*

  [ ]

DISCUSS

- What did you learn about knowing God? What results come from knowing Him?

- How does knowing God affect your response in the midst of difficult situations?

OBSERVE

Let's look again at the apostle Paul's response to suffering and what he told the Philippians about the result of knowing God.

PSALM 46:10

"Cease striving and know that I am God; I will be exalted among the nations, I will be exalted in the earth."

DANIEL 11:32B

…but the people who know their God will display strength and take action.

Supreme value to Christ (Paul)

Paul

Lord will give you peace to sleep

PHILIPPIANS 3:8-10

8 More than that, I count all things to be loss in view of the surpassing value of knowing Christ Jesus my Lord, for whom I have suffered the loss of all things, and count them but rubbish so that I may gain Christ,

9 and may be found in Him, not having a righteousness of my own derived from the Law, but that which is through faith in Christ, the righteousness which comes from God on the basis of faith,

10 that I may know Him and the power of His resurrection and the fellowship of His sufferings, being conformed to His death.

Leader: Read aloud Philippians 3:8-10. Have the group do the following:
- Circle all references to **Paul,** including pronouns.
- Draw a box around the words **know** and **knowing.**
- Underline **the actions of Paul** in these verses.

DISCUSS

- What did you learn from marking the references to Paul? What goals did he set for himself? How did this affect his response to suffering?

- What value did Paul place on knowing Christ?

- What importance do you place on knowing Christ?

- How is this reflected in the priorities of your daily life?

OBSERVE

We have seen that to believe God is to trust Him, and to do this effectively, we must truly know Him. What does the Bible reveal about God that enables us to place our confidence in Him?

Leader: Read aloud Isaiah 14:24,27; 46:9-10; and Psalm 138:8. Have the group…
- *mark all references to **God**, including pronouns, with a triangle:* △

Leader: Read aloud these same verses again and have the group…
- *underline **what God does** in these verses.*

DISCUSS

- What do you know about God from these verses?

ISAIAH 14:24,27

24 The LORD of hosts has sworn saying, "Surely, just as I have intended so it has happened, and just as I have planned so it will stand.

27 "For the LORD of hosts has planned, and who can frustrate it? And as for His stretched-out hand, who can turn it back?"

ISAIAH 46:9-10

9 "Remember the former things long past, for I am God, and there is no other; I am God, and there is no one like Me,

10 Declaring the end from the beginning, and from ancient times things which have not been done, saying, 'My

purpose will be estab-
lished, and I will
accomplish all My good
pleasure.'"

PSALM 138:8

The LORD will accom-
plish what concerns me;
Your lovingkindness, O
LORD, is everlasting; do
not forsake the works of
Your hands.

PSALM 139:1-6

¹ O LORD, You have
searched me and
known me.

² You know when I
sit down and when I
rise up; You understand
my thought from afar.

³ You scrutinize my
path and my lying
down, and are inti-
mately acquainted
with all my ways.

• How can understanding these truths
about God affect you when you are experiencing pain?

OBSERVE

*Leader: Read aloud Psalm 139:1-6. Have
the group…*

> • *mark with a triangle each reference to
> **the Lord:*** △
>
> • *draw a box around **know, under-
> stand**, and **knowledge:*** ☐

DISCUSS

• What did you learn about God in this
passage? What does God know and what
does He understand?

• How might knowing these truths about God help you deal with problems that are beyond your understanding?

OBSERVE

As both shepherd boy and king, David knew God intimately and trusted Him fully. Let's look at the psalm he sang after the Lord delivered him from the hand of his enemies.

Leader: Read aloud 2 Samuel 22:1-4. Have the group...

- *mark all references to **God** and **the Lord** with a triangle.*
- *underline **the actions of David** noted in these verses.*

---

4 Even before there is a word on my tongue, behold, O LORD, You know it all.

5 You have enclosed me behind and before, and laid Your hand upon me.

6 Such knowledge is too wonderful for me; it is too high, I cannot attain to it.

2 SAMUEL 22:1-4

1 And David spoke the words of this song to the LORD in the day that the LORD delivered him from the hand of all his enemies and from the hand of Saul.

2 He said, "The LORD is my rock and my fortress and my deliverer;

³ My God, my rock, in whom I take refuge, my shield and the horn of my salvation, my stronghold and my refuge; my savior, You save me from violence.

David

⁴ "I call upon the LORD, who is worthy to be praised, and I am saved from my enemies."

PSALM 107:19-20

¹⁹ Then they cried out to the LORD in their trouble; He saved them out of their distresses.

David

²⁰ He sent His word and healed them, and delivered them from their destructions.

DISCUSS

• What words did David use to describe God?

• How did David respond when his enemies attacked? What did God do for David?

• What did you learn from David's example about what enables us to deal with difficult situations and what we can expect God to do?

OBSERVE

Leader: *Read aloud Psalm 107:19-20. Have the group…*

- *mark with a star* ✡ *the pronouns **they** and **them,** which refer to the people of Israel in a time of distress.*
- *mark with a triangle the references to **the Lord:** △*

DISCUSS

• What did Israel do?

• How did God respond?

- If God responded in this way to Israel, His chosen people, what will God do for us, His church?

OBSERVE

Leader: *Read aloud Psalm 119:50.*
- *Have the group mark the word* **comfort** *with a* **C.**

PSALM 119:50

This is my comfort in my affliction, that Your word has revived me.

DISCUSS

- Where did the author of this psalm find comfort?

- What does this show you about where you can turn for comfort in your times of suffering?

OBSERVE

Leader: *Read aloud 2 Corinthians 1:3-4. Have the group…*
- *mark with a triangle the references to* **God:** △
- *mark each reference to* **comfort** *with a* **C.**

2 CORINTHIANS 1:3-4

3 Blessed be the God and Father of our Lord Jesus Christ, the Father of mercies and God of all comfort,

4 who comforts us in all our affliction so that we will be able to comfort those who are in any affliction with the comfort with which we ourselves are comforted by God.

DISCUSS

• What did you learn about God's role in providing comfort?

• What insight did you gain about your own suffering and the possible impact of your experience?

• How are we equipped to help others facing affliction?

ROMANS 8:28,37

28 And we know that God causes all things to work together for good to those who love God, to those who are called according to His purpose.

37 But in all these things we overwhelmingly conquer through Him who loved us.

OBSERVE

Leader: *Read aloud Romans 8:28,37; 2 Corinthians 2:14; and Jude 24.*

> • *Have the group say aloud and mark with a triangle all references to **God** and **Christ,** including the pronouns.*

DISCUSS

• According to these verses, what does God do for the believer?

- How can these truths encourage you when you are experiencing difficult times?

- Consider a challenge or trial you currently are facing. What truth or promise from these verses will you claim to help you endure?

OBSERVE

The night before He was crucified, Jesus prepared His disciples for the difficult days to come.

Leader: *Read aloud John 16:33. Have the group…*
- *underline each reference to **the world**.*
- *mark each reference to **Jesus**, who is speaking, with a cross.*

---

2 CORINTHIANS 2:14

But thanks be to God, who always leads us in His triumph in Christ, and manifests through us the sweet aroma of the knowledge of Him in every place.

Paul

JUDE 24

Now to Him who is able to keep you from stumbling, and to make you stand in the presence of His glory blameless with great joy.

Jude

JOHN 16:33

These things I have spoken to you, so that in Me you may have peace. In the world you have tribulation, but take courage; I have overcome the world.

Jesus

DISCUSS

• What did Jesus warn His disciples to expect from the world?

• What encouragement did He offer to the disciples—and to you?

1 JOHN 5:4-5

4 For whatever is born of God overcomes the world; and this is the victory that has overcome the world—our faith.

5 Who is the one who overcomes the world, but he who believes that Jesus is the Son of God?

OBSERVE

***Leader:** Read aloud 1 John 5:4-5.*

• Have the group draw a cloud shape like this ⌢⌣ *around **overcome the world**.*

DISCUSS

• According to the verses you just read in 1 John 5:4-5, what characteristic defines those who overcome the world?

• How is the world overcome?

INSIGHT

The word *faith* in this passage is translated from the Greek word *pistis*. According to W.E. Vines, the main elements of faith are:

- a firm conviction producing a full acknowledgement of God's revelation or truth
- a personal surrender to Him
- a conduct inspired by such surrender

• In light of this definition, is faith synonymous with knowledge? Is it sufficient to merely say "I believe"?

• How does what we learn about faith and overcoming shape our response to difficult times?

WRAP IT UP

Our study this week has examined how to follow Jesus' instruction to not have a troubled heart. We are to put our trust in God, who is our strength in time of trouble. He is the One we are to run to for safety. He is the One who will give us peace in the midst of the storm.

The more we know Him—and know what He does for us—the more convinced we become that He is able to heal us, comfort us, and equip us to walk victoriously.

To be an overcomer when our world seems to be falling down all around us, we must believe God's Word, surrender our lives to it, and live in ways that reflect His truth.

Where do you run when you have trouble? Who are you trusting? Do you place a high value on knowing God and knowing His Word? Is what you believe reflected in your response to the stresses and troubles you face?

WEEK SIX

God doesn't just call us to endure suffering with faith; He gives us instructions and examples to equip us for the challenge. In His Word we find all the wisdom we need to walk victoriously through the trials of life.

We will begin the final lesson of our study by examining how King Jehoshaphat dealt with a great challenge in his life. His example will give us insights for handling the difficulties that come into our lives.

OBSERVE

Leader: Read aloud 2 Chronicles 20:2-12. Have the group do the following:

- *Circle each reference to **Jehoshaphat**, including pronouns:* ◯
- *Mark each reference to **God**, including pronouns, with a triangle:* △

DISCUSS

- According to verse 2, what difficulty did Jehoshaphat face?

- According to verses 3 and 4, how did Jehoshaphat feel and what did he do in this difficult time?

2 CHRONICLES 20:2-12

2 Then some came and reported to Jehoshaphat, saying, "A great multitude is coming against you from beyond the sea, out of Aram and behold, they are in Hazazon-tamar (that is Engedi)."

3 Jehoshaphat was afraid and turned his attention to seek the LORD, and proclaimed a fast throughout all Judah.

4 So Judah gathered together to seek help from the LORD; they

even came from all the cities of Judah to seek the LORD.

5 Then Jehoshaphat stood in the assembly of Judah and Jerusalem, in the house of the LORD before the new court,

6 and he said, "O LORD, the God of our fathers, are You not God in the heavens? And are You not ruler over all the kingdoms of the nations? Power and might are in Your hand so that no one can stand against You.

7 "Did You not, O our God, drive out the inhabitants of this land before Your people Israel and give it to the descendants of Abraham Your friend forever?

• Beginning with verse 5, move through the text verse by verse. Discuss what Jehoshaphat knew about God that motivated him to seek the Lord in his trouble. Discuss how the knowledge of these truths fit your own situation.

Fear motivated him
He Trusted God

- What principles from Jehoshaphat's actions can help you deal with difficult situations?

8 "They have lived in it, and have built You a sanctuary there for Your name, saying,

9 'Should evil come upon us, the sword, or judgment, or pestilence, or famine, we will stand before this house and before You (for Your name is in this house) and cry to You in our distress, and You will hear and deliver us.'

10 "Now behold, the sons of Ammon and Moab and Mount Seir, whom You did not let Israel invade when they came out of the land of Egypt (they turned aside from them and did not destroy them),

11 see how they are rewarding us by coming to drive us out

from Your possession which You have given us as an inheritance.

12 "O our God, will You not judge them? For we are powerless before this great multitude who are coming against us; nor do we know what to do, but our eyes are on You."

2 CHRONICLES 20:13-19

13 All Judah was standing before the LORD, with their infants, their wives and their children.

14 Then in the midst of the assembly the Spirit of the LORD came upon Jahaziel the son of Zechariah, the son of Benaiah, the son of Jeiel, the son of Mattaniah, the Levite of the sons of Asaph;

• According to verse 12, how did Jehoshaphat conclude his prayer?

*Powerless
Admit your
weakness*

OBSERVE

Leader: *Let's continue our study of 2 Chronicles 20:13-19. Have the group…*

> • *circle each reference to **Jehoshaphat**, including pronouns:* ◯
> • *mark each reference to **the Lord** with a triangle:* △

Leader: *Read aloud 2 Chronicles 20:13-19 once more.*

> • *Have the group underline **the instructions** given in this passage, those things the people are to do and not to do.*

DISCUSS

• What was God's message to Judah, Jerusalem, and the king?

• What promise or assurance does God give them in verses 15 and 17?

• How did Jehoshaphat, Judah, and Jerusalem respond to the message from God?

• What principles can you apply from 2 Chronicles 20 to your battles in life?

15 and he said, "Listen, all Judah and the inhabitants of Jerusalem and King Jehoshaphat, thus says the LORD to you, 'Do not fear or be dismayed because of this great multitude, for the battle is not yours, but God's.

16 'Tomorrow go down against them. Behold, they will come up by the ascent of Ziz, and you will find them at the end of the valley in front of the wilderness of Jeruel.

17 'You need not fight in this battle; station yourselves, stand and see the salvation of the LORD on your behalf, O Judah and Jerusalem.' Do not fear or be dismayed;

tomorrow go out to face them, for the LORD is with you."

18 Jehoshaphat bowed his head with his face to the ground, and all Judah and the inhabitants of Jerusalem fell down before the LORD, worshiping the LORD.

19 The Levites, from the sons of the Kohathites and of the sons of the Korahites, stood up to praise the LORD God of Israel, with a very loud voice.

2 CHRONICLES 20:20-24

20 They rose early in the morning and went out to the wilderness of Tekoa; and when they went out Jehoshaphat stood and said, "Listen to me, O Judah and inhabitants of

OBSERVE

Let's continue our study of 2 Chronicles to see what follows God's message to Jehoshaphat and his people.

Leader: Read aloud 2 Chronicles 20:20-24. Have the group…

- *circle the references to **Jehoshaphat, Judah,** and **the inhabitants of Jerusalem,** including pronouns.*
- *mark each reference to **destroy** or **destroying** with an **X.***

DISCUSS

- What did you learn from marking references to Jehoshaphat, Judah, and Jerusalem?

- In what way did God fulfill His Word to Judah?

He fullfilled his promise

• How was the defeat of Ammon, Moab, and Mount Seir accomplished?

• Summarize what you have learned from Jehoshaphat and Judah's example about how to deal with life's difficulties and disappointments.

Jerusalem, put your trust in the LORD your God, and you will be established. Put your trust in His prophets and succeed."

21 When he had consulted with the people, he appointed those who sang to the LORD and those who praised Him in holy attire, as they went out before the army and said, "Give thanks to the LORD, for His lovingkindness is everlasting."

22 When they began singing and praising, the LORD set ambushes against the sons of Ammon, Moab and Mount Seir, who had come against Judah; so they were routed.

23 For the sons of Ammon and Moab rose up against the inhabitants of Mount Seir destroying them completely; and when they had finished with the inhabitants of Seir, they helped to destroy one another.

24 When Judah came to the lookout of the wilderness, they looked toward the multitude, and behold, they were corpses lying on the ground, and no one had escaped.

Joshua 1:7-9

7 "Only be strong and very courageous; be careful to do according to all the law which Moses My servant commanded you; do not turn from it to the

OBSERVE

Let's look at a passage of God's instructions to Joshua as he prepared to lead Israel into the Promised Land, knowing they would have to face the enemy.

Leader: Read aloud Joshua 1:7-9.

*• Have the group underline **the instructions** given to Joshua in this passage.*

INSIGHT

The Hebrew word for *prosperous* in verse 8 is *tsalach,* which, in this context, means "you will accomplish what God desires."

The Hebrew word for *dismayed* in verse 9 is *chathath,* which means "to be broken down by violence, confusion; fear; to panic or to be discouraged."

The Hebrew word for *strong* in verse 7 is *chazaq,* which means "to fasten, to seize, to get a grip on."

The Hebrew word for *courageous* in verse 9 is *amats,* which means "to be alert physically and mentally, to not fall apart."

DISCUSS

• What did you learn from marking the instructions in this passage?

• How do the definitions in the Insight box enhance your understanding of these instructions?

• According to verse 8, what is the result of obeying God's commands?

• How can living by these instructions make a difference when you are in a difficult situation?

OBSERVE

Now let's turn to some New Testament verses, written by the apostle Paul, that show us how to keep our minds focused on God in the midst of difficult situations. What we do with our thoughts can greatly impact how we handle the trials in our lives.

right or to the left, so that you may have success wherever you go.

8 "This book of the law shall not depart from your mouth, but you shall meditate on it day and night, so that you may be careful to do according to all that is written in it; for then you will make your way prosperous, and then you will have success.

9 "Have I not commanded you? Be strong and courageous! Do not tremble or be dismayed, for the LORD your God is with you wherever you go."

2 CORINTHIANS 4:16-18

16 Therefore we do not lost heart, but though our outer man

is decaying, yet <u>our</u> inner man is being renewed day by day.

17 For momentary, light affliction is producing for us an eternal weight of glory far beyond all comparison,

18 while we look not at the things which are seen, but at the things which are not seen; for the things which are seen are temporal, but the things which are not seen are eternal.

2 Corinthians 10:5

We are destroying speculations and every lofty thing raised up against the knowledge of God, and we are taking every thought captive to the obedience of Christ.

Leader: Read aloud 2 Corinthians 4:16-18.
  • *Circle each reference to* **Paul.** *(The plural pronouns* **we** *and* **us** *refer to Paul and Timothy.)*
  • *Draw a slash (/) between phrases in which Paul shows* **a contrast between two things.** *(Look for words like "but" and "yet.")*

DISCUSS

• What did Paul do that enabled him to not lose heart as he endured suffering?

• What did you learn from marking the contrasts? How can this guide your attitude and actions when dealing with trials?

OBSERVE

Leader: Read aloud 2 Corinthians 10:5; Colossians 3:1-2; and Philippians 4:8.
  • *Have the group underline each* **instruction** *or* **what the believer is already doing.**

DISCUSS

• What do all these verses have in common?

• According to these verses, what is the believer instructed to do?

• How would living by these truths enable you to live victoriously in the midst of trials and challenges in your daily life?

OBSERVE

Leader: *Read aloud Hebrews 4:16, reprinted for you on the following page.*

> • *Have the group underline each instruction.*

COLOSSIANS 3:1-2

1 Therefore if you have been raised up with Christ, keep seeking the things above, where Christ is, seated at the right hand of God.

2 Set your mind on the things above, not on the things that are on earth.

PHILIPPIANS 4:8

Finally, brethren, whatever is true, whatever is honorable, whatever is right, whatever is pure, whatever is lovely, whatever is of good repute, if there is any excellence and if anything worthy of praise, dwell on these things.

Hebrews 4:16

Therefore let us draw near with confidence to the throne of grace, so that we may receive mercy and find grace to help in time of need.

INSIGHT

The phrase *draw near* in the Greek is in the present tense, which indicates that we should continually, as a habit of our lives, draw near to the throne of grace.

Grace is translated from the Greek word c*haris*. It refers to the favor of God that not only turns us to Christ for salvation, but also strengthens us and enables us to live victoriously in all circumstances of life.

DISCUSS

• What are we instructed to do?

• What will be the benefit of doing this?

• According to the explanations in the Insight box, how are we to live in the light of these truths?

• Discuss what God has shown you through the principles in this study that can make a difference in the way you live through difficult times.

WRAP IT UP

When you find yourself in the midst of a trial and it seems everything is going wrong, what are you to do? Instead of focusing on your circumstances, turn your attention to God.

Every believer is to have an eternal perspective. We are to take every thought captive, believe in God, and obey His Word. We are to praise and acknowledge who God is and what He has done for us. The Word of God should have priority in our lives. We are to meditate on it and be obedient to it.

As the lives of Jehoshaphat and Paul demonstrate, we do not have to lose heart, no matter what trials or pain we encounter. Through God's grace, we have everything we need to be strong and courageous and not fear. All we have to do is believe and act on these truths:

- The promises of God and the Word never change.
- The battle is not ours, but the Lord's.
- The Lord is with us.
- The Lord will not fail us.
- The Lord will not forsake us.

When we draw near to God, He is always ready to welcome us with outstretched arms. He will pour out His mercy and comfort and give us His enabling strength and power to walk through whatever happens in our lives.

When pain, suffering, persecution, and trials come, what will you do? Will you trust in yourself and what you can do? Or will you trust in the One who is able to do exceedingly, abundantly above what you could ask or think?

When you seem to have no strength of your own, that's when you can most fully rest in the One whose strength is made perfect in your weakness.

40 MINUTE BIBLE STUDIES

No-Homeworl
That Help Yo

A 6-WEEK, NO-HOMEWORK BIBLE STUDY
MORE THAN 700,000 SOLD IN THE SERIES

Being a Disciple:
Counting the
Real Cost

Kay Arthur, Tom & Jane Hart

PRECEPT MINISTRIES INTERNATIONAL

A 6-WEEK, NO-HOMEWORK BIBLE STUDY
MORE THAN 700,000 SOLD IN THE SERIES

Having a Real
Relationship
with God

Kay Arthur

PRECEPT MINISTRIES INTERNATIONAL

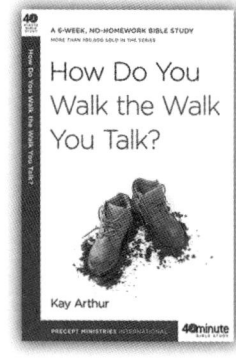

A 6-WEEK, NO-HOMEWORK BIBLE STUDY
MORE THAN 700,000 SOLD IN THE SERIES

How Do You
Walk the Walk
You Talk?

Kay Arthur

PRECEPT MINISTRIES INTERNATIONAL

A 6-WEEK, NO-HOMEWORK BIBLE STUDY
MORE THAN 700,000 SOLD IN THE SERIES

Living a
Life of
True Worship

Kay Arthur, Bob & Diane Vereen

PRECEPT MINISTRIES INTERNATIONAL

A 6-WEEK, NO-HOMEWORK BIBLE STUDY
MORE THAN 700,000 SOLD IN THE SERIES

Living
Victoriously in
Difficult Times

Kay Arthur, Bob & Diane Vereen

PRECEPT MINISTRIES INTERNATIONAL

A 6-WEEK, NO-HOMEWORK BIBLE STUDY
MORE THAN 700,000 SOLD IN THE SERIES

How to Make
Choices You
Won't Regret

Kay Arthur, David & BJ Lawson

PRECEPT MINISTRIES INTERNATIONAL

A 6-WEEK, NO-HOMEWORK BIBLE STUDY
MORE THAN 700,000 SOLD IN THE SERIES

Money and
Possessions:
The Quest for
Contentment

Kay Arthur & David Arthur

PRECEPT MINISTRIES INTERNATIONAL

A 6-WEEK, NO-HOMEWORK BIBLE STUDY
MORE THAN 700,000 SOLD IN THE SERIES

Building a
Marriage That
Really Works

Kay Arthur, David & BJ Lawson

PRECEPT MINISTRIES INTERNATIONAL

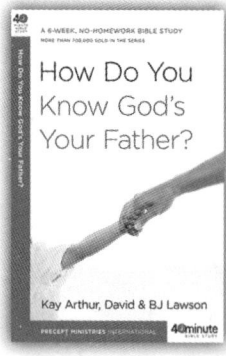

A 6-WEEK, NO-HOMEWORK BIBLE STUDY
MORE THAN 700,000 SOLD IN THE SERIES

How Do You
Know God's
Your Father?

Kay Arthur, David & BJ Lawson

PRECEPT MINISTRIES INTERNATIONAL

Bible Studies
Discover Truth For Yourself

 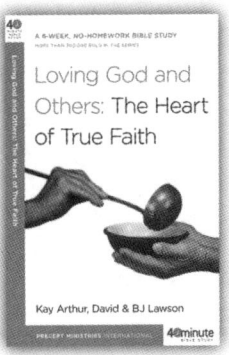 

Also Available:

A Man's Strategy for Conquering Temptation

Rising to the Call of Leadership

Key Principles of Biblical Fasting

What Does the Bible Say About Sex?

Turning Your Heart Toward God

Fatal Distractions: Conquering Destructive Temptations

Spiritual Warfare: Overcoming the Enemy

Another powerful study series
from beloved Bible teacher

KAY ARTHUR

The Lord series provides insightful, warm-hearted Bible studies designed to meet you where you are —and help you discover God's answers to your deepest needs.

ALSO AVAILABLE:
One-year devotionals to draw you closer to the heart of God.

ABOUT THE AUTHORS AND PRECEPT MINISTRIES INTERNATIONAL

KAY ARTHUR is known around the world as an international Bible teacher, author, conference speaker, and host of the national radio and television programs *Precepts for Life,* which reaches a worldwide viewing audience of over 94 million. A four-time Gold Medallion Award–winning author, Kay has authored more than 100 books and Bible studies.

Kay and her husband, Jack, founded Precept Ministries International in 1970 in Chattanooga, Tennessee, with a vision to establish people in God's Word. Today, the ministry has a worldwide outreach. In addition to inductive study training workshops and thousands of small-group studies across America, PMI reaches nearly 150 countries with inductive Bible studies translated into nearly 70 languages, teaching people to discover Truth for themselves.

BOB AND DIANE VEREEN serve as ambassadors-at-large for Precept Ministries International, speaking at conferences around the world and overseeing a number of Precept's international offices. They both travel the globe teaching people how to study the Bible inductively as well as mentoring and training national leadership. They have been on staff since 1991, following sixteen years of prior involvement with Precept Ministries International. Bob was a contributor to *The New Inductive Study Bible* and has written for the New Inductive Study Series and the 40-Minute Bible Studies series.

Contact Precept Ministries International for more information about inductive Bible studies in your area.

Precept Ministries International
P.O. Box 182218
Chattanooga, TN 37422-7218
800-763-8280
www.precept.org